THE
HOLINESS

CHARLES SPURGEON

 Whitaker House

All Scripture quotations are from the *King James Version* (KJV) of the Bible.

THE KEY TO HOLINESS

ISBN: 0-88368-409-8
Printed in the United States of America
Copyright © 1997 by Whitaker House

Whitaker House
30 Hunt Valley Circle
New Kensington, PA 15068

3 4 5 6 7 8 9 10 11 12 / 07 06 05 04 03 02 01 00

Contents

Chapter One

Perfection in Faith

*The LORD will perfect that which
concerneth me: thy mercy, O LORD,
endureth for ever: forsake not the
works of thine own hands.*
—Psalm 138:8

*For by one offering he hath perfected
for ever them that are sanctified.*
—Hebrews 10:14

Think for a moment about the preceding Scriptures. In the first Scripture, Psalm 138:8, David went from bold faith to meek prayer. After having said in confidence, "The LORD will perfect that which concerneth me," he was inclined to ask the Lord, "Forsake not the works of thine own hands," sinking, as it were, to a lower note in the scale of music. We, also, are often inclined in this way. We often behold perfection in the dim obscurity of the future, like the sun veiled behind a cloud. Our faith rests on it as a thing unseen at the present time; our hearts yearn for it as an inheritance still in reserve for us.

Yet, this perfection is brought near to us as a thing accomplished, as an ever present fact, whose eternal reality shines upon us with unclouded luster. It is because of this that I quote the verse, "By one offering [our Lord Jesus Christ] hath perfected for ever them that are sanctified" (Heb. 10:14). Is it not incredibly pleasing to observe that what is presented to us in one part of Scripture as a matter of *faith*, is stated in another place as a matter of *fact?* He has perfected us forever.

I have been turning this text over and over in my mind, and praying about it, and looking into it, and seeking illumination from the Holy Spirit; but it has taken me a long time to be clear about its exact meaning. It is very easy to select a meaning, and then to say, "That is what the text means"; and it is very easy also to look at something that lies upon the surface. However, I am not quite so sure that, after several hours of meditation, any believer would be able to ascertain what is the Spirit's mind in this particular verse, "By one offering [Christ] hath perfected for ever them that are sanctified."

When I was trying to find out what this meant, I thought I would simply read the chapters before it, and if I should happen to find any word that seemed to be the key to this verse, I would then, under the Spirit's guidance, seek to open this lock and mystery with the key that was there provided for me. Well, I read the chapters in Hebrews, and I did find something that seemed to explain the meaning of this verse. Now, as I write this chapter, I will try to show you what I think it means; and then I think it will stand out in a very clear and glorious light.

Sanctified as a Child of God

First, I will discuss the condition of the child of God—what he is. He is a sanctified person. The term *sanctified* is wholly intended for the children of God; they are described as sanctified people. What does this mean?

We usually say there are two meanings to the term *sanctified*. One is "set apart." God has set apart His people from before the foundation of the world (Eph. 1:4), to be His chosen and peculiar inheritance (Ps. 33:12), and we are sanctified by God the Father. The other meaning implies not the decree of the Father, but the work of the Holy Spirit. We are sanctified in

9

Christ Jesus, by the Holy Spirit, when He subdues our corruptions, imparts graces to us, and leads us onward in the divine walk and life of faith. Even so, the verse here, I think, includes both of these senses; and I must try, if I can, to find an illustration that will embrace them both.

What was the apostle writing about? In the ninth chapter of Hebrews, he wrote about the tabernacle, the candlestick, the table, the showbread, the sanctuary, the golden censer,[1] the ark of the covenant overlaid with gold, and the golden pot of manna (vv. 2–4). He also wrote about priests, and about priestly things and holy things (vv. 6–7). He declared that all these were sanctified things, but even though they were sanctified, they still needed to be made perfect by the sprinkling of blood (v. 7).

Now, I believe that the sanctification referred to in our text is to be understood in this sense. There were certain golden vessels that were used in the sanctuary, that were never used for anything else except the service of God. They were set apart; they were made holy; and they were kept strictly to be the vessels of the sanctuary of the Lord God. They were sanctified things.

---

[1]Censer: a vessel for burning incense.

In the sanctuary, there were people who did nothing else but wait upon the Lord. These people were chosen, and then they were prepared. God chose the tribe of Levi, and out of the tribe of Levi, He chose the house of Aaron. The members of Aaron's family were consecrated to their offices. They underwent certain ceremonies and various washings, and so they were made ceremonially holy; and these priests were therefore sanctified people because they were set apart, dedicated, and reserved for the special service of the Lord God. Now, that is just what you and I are, and what we ought to be: we are sanctified persons. That is to say, we are chosen by God to be the particular vessels that He will use in pouring out His mercy, and to be the special priests whom He will employ in His divine worship in this world.

No man had any right to take wine, for his own drinking, out of the golden cups of the sanctuary. If he did so, he did it to his own destruction—witness what happened to Belshazzar. (See Daniel 5.) He took the cups and the golden candlesticks, and so forth, and used them in his debaucheries, and lo! he was swept away, and the handwriting on the wall foretold his doom. In the same manner, Christian men are not to be used for anything but for God. They are a people set apart (Ps. 4:3); they are vessels of mercy (see Romans 9:23); they are not for the Devil's use, not for their own use, not for the world's use, but for their Master's use. He has purposefully made them to be used entirely, solely, and wholly for Him.

Now, that is what is meant in this text by the word *sanctified*. We are sanctified people, set apart for God's use, consecrated just as the vessels, the cups, the candlesticks, the tables, and the altars of the sanctuary, were sanctified unto God and set apart for His service. We are priests, and we are sanctified, but not because of any holiness in our character, just as there were some of those early priests who were not holy in their character.

My text does not concern character. Rather, it concerns our position in the sight of God. We are not perfect in character, any one of us; we are only perfect in position. There were two men who officiated as priests before God, namely, the sons of Eli, who committed sin and iniquity before God. (See 1 Samuel 2:22.) And yet, they were set apart for God's service, for when they offered the sacrifices as priests, they were officially accepted as being sanctified persons because they had been washed with water and sprinkled with blood.

Now, dear reader, the children of God are sanctified people, sanctified to offer spiritual sacrifices to God through Jesus Christ, and we have no right to do anything else but serve God. "What," you say, "am I not to attend to my business?" Yes, and you are to serve God in your business. "Am I not to look after my family?" Assuredly, you are, and you are to serve God in looking after your family, but still you are to be set apart.

You are not to wear the white robe nor the breastplate (see Exodus 28:4), but still you are to think of yourself as being as much a priest as if the breastplate were on your breast, and the white robe about your loins; for you are "priests unto God and his Father" (Rev. 1:6). He has made you a peculiar generation and a royal priesthood (see 1 Peter 2:9), and He has set you apart for Himself (Ps. 4:3).

Now, I think that this first point has given you an idea of what the rest must mean. I have already hinted at what I think is the sense of the text. I have explained clearly enough, I suppose, in what sense God's people are sanctified people, as understood in this verse. They are chosen and set apart and reserved to be God's instruments and God's servants, and, therefore, they are sanctified.

Perfected in Christ's Blood

Now comes the second thing. "He hath perfected for ever them that are sanctified" (Heb. 10:14). In what sense are we to understand that Christ has perfected these who are sanctified? Why, in the sense of what Christ has done for them. When the golden vessels were brought into the temple or into the sanctuary, they were sanctified the very first moment that they were dedicated to God. No one dared to employ them for anything except holy uses. Even so, they were not perfect. What did they need, then, to make them perfect? They needed to have blood sprinkled on them; and, as soon as the blood was sprinkled on them, those golden vessels were perfect vessels, officially perfect. God accepted them as being holy and perfect things, and they stood in His sight as instruments of an acceptable worship.

It was the same with the Levites and the priests. As soon as they were set apart to their office—as soon as they were born, in fact— they were consecrated; they belonged to God; they were His peculiar priesthood. However, they were not perfect until they had passed through many washings, and had had the blood sprinkled upon them. Then God looked upon them, in their official priestly character,

14

as being perfect. I repeat, they were not perfect in character; they were only perfect officially, perfect in the sight of God, and they stood before Him to offer sacrifice as acceptably as if they had been as pure as Adam himself.

Now, then, how does this refer to us, and what is the meaning of this text, that "by one offering he hath perfected for ever them that are sanctified" (Heb. 10:14)? Turn back to Hebrews 9:6–7, where you will read,

> *Now when these things were thus ordained, the priests went always into the first tabernacle, accomplishing the service of God. But into the second went the high priest alone once every year, not without blood, which he offered for himself, and for the errors of the people.*

Note that the first meaning of my text is this: the child of God is a priest, and as a priest he is sanctified to enter within the veil. He is now permitted to go into the place that was once within the veil, but that is not so now because the veil is torn in two. (See Matthew 27:51.)

The high priest, on the contrary, could not go within the veil, because he was not perfect. He had to be sprinkled with the blood, and that made him officially perfect. It would not make him perfect merely to put on the breastplate, or to wear the ephod; he was not perfect until the blood had been sprinkled upon him, and then he went within the veil. Even so, when the next year came around, he was not fit to go within the veil until blood was sprinkled on him again. The same would happen every year, for although he was always a sanctified man, he was not always, officially, a perfect man. He had to be sprinkled with blood again. And so, year after year, the high priest who went within the veil needed afresh to be made perfect, in order to obtain access to God.

A Position of Perfection

Therefore, this is one sense of Hebrews 10:14. The apostle said that we who are the priests of God have a right as priests to go to God's mercy seat, which is within the veil; but it would mean our death to go there unless we were perfect. However, we are perfect, for the blood of Christ has been sprinkled on us, and, therefore, our standing before God is the standing of perfection. Our standing, in our own conscience, is imperfection, just as the character of the priest might be imperfect. But that has nothing to do with it. Our standing in the sight of God is a standing of perfection; and when He sees the blood—as of old, when the destroying angel passed over Israel (see Exodus 12:3–13)—so this day, when He sees the blood, God passes over our sins and accepts us at the throne of His mercy, as if we were perfect.

Therefore, let us come boldly to His throne (Heb. 4:16).

> *Let us draw near with a true heart in full assurance of faith, having our hearts sprinkled from an evil conscience, and our bodies washed with pure water.*
> *(Heb. 10:22)*

In this twenty-second verse of Hebrews 10, the apostle brought in one inference that I have just drawn from my text: in having access to God, perfection is absolutely necessary. God cannot talk with an imperfect being. He could talk with Adam in the Garden, but He could not talk with you or with me, even in Paradise itself, as imperfect creatures.

How, then, are we to have fellowship with God, and access to His throne? Why, simply through the blood of Christ, which "hath perfected for ever them that are sanctified" (Heb. 10:14). As a consequence of His offering, we can come boldly to the throne of heavenly grace, and may come boldly in all our times of need (Heb. 4:16). And, what is better still, we are always perfect, always fit to come to the throne, whatever our doubts, whatever our sins.

I say this not of the priest's character; we have nothing to do with that at present. We come before God in our position, in our standing, not in our character; and therefore, we may come as perfect men at all times, knowing that God sees no sin in Jacob, and no iniquity in Israel. (See Micah 3:8.) For in this sense, Christ has perfected forever every consecrated vessel of His mercy.

Is this not a delightful thought, that when I come before the throne of God, I feel that I am a sinner, but God does not look upon me as one? When I approach Him to offer my thanksgivings, I feel that I am unworthy in myself, but I am not unworthy in that official standing in which He has placed me. As a sanctified and perfected being in Christ, I have the blood upon me. God regards me in my sacrifice, in my worship, yes, and in myself, too, as being perfect.

Oh, how joyful this is! And there is no need to repeat this perfecting a second time. It is an everlasting perfection; it allows a constant access to the throne of heavenly grace. That is one meaning of the text.

Perfection in Faith

Perfected Forever

A little further on, the apostle, in Hebrews 9:21, wrote, "He sprinkled with blood both the tabernacle, and all the vessels of the ministry." They were all sanctified vessels, as you know, but they were not perfect vessels until they were sprinkled with the blood.

> And almost all things are by the law purged with blood; and without shedding of blood is no remission. It was therefore necessary that the patterns of things in the heavens should be purified with these; but the heavenly things themselves with better sacrifices than these.　　　　(Heb. 9:22–23)

Now, the vessels of the sanctuary, as I have said, were sanctified the moment they were put there, but they were not perfect. God could not therefore accept any sacrifice that was touched with the golden tongs or that lay upon the bronze altar, as long as those golden tongs and the bronze altar were imperfect. What was done to make them perfect? Why, they were sprinkled with blood; but they had to be sprinkled with blood many, many times—once, twice, three times, multitudes of times—because they continually needed to be made perfect.

You and I, if we are consecrated people, are presently like the vessels of the sanctuary. Sometimes we are like the censer: God fills us with joy, and then the smoke of incense ascends from us. Sometimes we are like the slaughter knife that the priest used: we are enabled to deny our lusts, to deny ourselves, and to put the knife to the neck of the victim. And sometimes we are like the altar: upon us God is pleased to lay a sacrifice of labor, and there it smokes acceptably to heaven. We are made like sanctified things of His house.

But, beloved, although we are sanctified and He has chosen us to be the vessels of His spiritual temple, we are not perfect until the blood is on us. Yet, blessed be His name, that blood has been put upon us once, and we are perfected for eternity. Is it not delightful to think that when God uses us in His service, He could not use unhallowed instruments? The Lord God is so pure that He could not use anything but a perfect tool to work with.

"Then surely He could never use you or me," you say. No! Do you not see? The blood is on us, and we are the sanctified instruments of His grace; moreover, we are the perfect instruments of His grace through the blood of Jesus. Oh! I take delight in just thinking about it! I am imperfect in my own estimation and, rightly enough, in yours; yet, when God makes use of me, He does not make use of an imperfect man. No, He looks upon me as being perfect in Christ, and then He says, "I can use this tool. I could not put My hand to an unholy thing, but I will look upon him as being perfected forever in Christ, and therefore I can use him."

Oh, Christian, do try to digest this precious thought. It has indeed been precious to my soul since I first laid hold of it. You cannot tell what God may do with you, because if He uses you at all, He does not use you as a sinner. Rather, He uses you as a sanctified person; no, more than that, He uses you as a perfect person. I will repeat it: I do not see how a holy God could use an unholy instrument; but He puts the blood on us, and then He makes us perfect—He perfects us for eternity—and then He uses us.

And so, we may see the work of God carried on by men who we think are imperfect, but, in reality, we never see God doing any of His deeds except with a perfect instrument. If you were to ask me how He has done it, I would tell you that all His consecrated ones, all whom He has sanctified to His use, He has first of all perfected forever through the sacrifice of Jesus Christ.

A Perfect Justification before God

And now we will examine one more thought, and then I will have given you the full meaning of Hebrews 10:14. In Hebrews 7:19, there is a word that is a key to the meaning of my text, and that helped me through it:

> *For the law made nothing perfect, but the bringing in of a better hope **did**; by the which we draw nigh unto God.*
>
> *(emphasis added)*

Compare Hebrews 10:1:

> *The law having a shadow of good things to come, and not the very image of the things, can never with those sacrifices which they offered year by year continually make the comers thereunto perfect.*

There is the word *perfect,* which is implied in the verse that follows: "For then [if they had been perfect] would they not have ceased to be offered?" (v. 2). Why offer any more, if you are already a perfect man? Because, if the sacrifice is perfect, "the worshippers once purged should have had no more conscience of sins" (v. 2).

Note that the Jewish sacrifice was never
intended to make the Jews' moral character
any better, and it did not. It had no effect upon
what we call a person's sanctification. All the
sacrifice dealt with was his justification; and
after that, the perfection would be sought. The
perfection is not of sanctification, which the
Arminian[2] talks about. Rather, it is the perfection of official standing, as a person stands justified before God.

Now, that is the meaning of the word *perfect* here. It does not mean that the sacrifice
did not make the man perfectly holy, perfectly
moral, and so forth, because the sacrifice had
no tendency to do that, for it was quite another
matter. Rather, it means that it did not perfectly make him justified in his own conscience
and in the sight of God, because he had to
come and offer again.

Suppose a man who is troubled in his conscience comes sighing to the temple, and he
must speak to the priest. He says to the priest,
"I have committed such and such a sin."

"Ah!" says the priest. "You will never have
any ease in your conscience unless you bring a

---

[2]Arminian: one who is opposed to the absolute predestination of
strict Calvinism and who maintains the possibility of salvation
for all.

sin offering." So the man brings a sin offering, and it is offered, and the man sees it burn, and he goes away. He has faith—faith in the great Sin Offering that is to come—and his conscience is easy.

A day or two later, the same feelings arise; and what does he do? He goes to the priest again. "Ah!" says the priest. "You must bring another offering; you must bring a trespass offering." So, he brings the trespass offering, and his conscience grows easier for a time; but the more his conscience comes alive, the more he sees the unsatisfactory character of the offering he brings. At last, he says, "I am so uneasy; how I wish that I could have a sacrifice every hour! For when I put my hand on the head of the victim, I feel so happy; when I come to see it slaughtered, and the blood flowing, I feel so easy; but I do not feel perfect. I will go up to the temple again, so that I may live."

So he sees a lamb slaughtered in the morning, and tears of joy are in his eyes. "Oh!" he says. "I have seen that lamb; and when I saw the blood of that lamb flowing, I felt so glad." Noon comes. "Ah!" he says. "My sins arise again; where can I get relief for my conscience?" So off he goes to the temple. And there is another lamb in the evening, because

God well knew that the sacrifices were themselves imperfect—only a shadow of the great Substance—and that His people would need to have the service renewed, not only every year, but every day—no, every morning and every evening.

But now, beloved, behold the glory of Christ Jesus as revealed to us in our text. Those sacrifices could not "make the comers thereunto perfect" (Heb. 10:1). They could not feel in their own conscience that they were perfectly justified, and they wanted fresh offerings; but today we see the slaughtered Lamb on Calvary. It may have been just yesterday that you rejoiced in Him, but you can rejoice in Him again today.

Years ago, I sought Him, and I found Him. I do not want another Lamb. I do not want another sacrifice. I can still see that blood flowing, and I can feel continually that I have no more consciousness of sin. The sins are gone. I have no more remembrance of them; I am purged from them; and as I see the perpetually flowing blood of Calvary, and the ever rising merits of His glorious passion, I am compelled to rejoice in this fact, that He has perfected me forever (Heb. 10:14). He has made me completely perfect through His sacrifice.

And now, Christian, try to lay hold of this meaning of the text. Christ has set your conscience at ease forever; and if it disturbs you, recall that it has no cause to do so, if you are a believer in Christ. For has He not given you that which will put away all consciousness of sin? Oh, rejoice! His sacrifice has purged you so entirely that you may sit down and rest. You may sing with the poet—

> Turn, then, my soul unto thy rest;
> The merits of thy great High Priest
>   Speak peace and liberty.
> Trust in his efficacious blood,
> Nor fear thy banishment from God,
>   Since Jesus died for thee.

Look again at Hebrews 10:14. Once again, I am going to repeat the same things, lest I should not be quite understood. We, as believers, cannot have access to God unless it is on the footing of perfection; for God cannot walk and talk with imperfect creatures. But, we are perfect—not in character, of course, for we are still sinners—but we are perfected through the blood of Jesus Christ, so that God can allow us as perfected creatures to have access to Him. We may come boldly to the throne of grace (Heb. 4:16), because, being sprinkled with the blood, God does not look on us as unholy and unclean. Otherwise, He could not allow us to come to His mercy seat. However, He looks upon us as being perfected forever through the one sacrifice of Christ.

That is one thing. Another is this: we are the vessels of God's temple; He has chosen us to be like the golden pots of His sanctuary. Those vessels, remember, were made perfect by being sprinkled with blood. God could never accept a worship offered to Him in unholy vessels. Likewise, God could not accept the praise that comes from your unholy heart; He could not accept the song that springs from your uncircumcised lips, nor the faith that arises from your doubting soul, unless He had taken the great precaution to sprinkle you with the blood of Christ. And now, whatever He uses you for, He uses you as a perfect instrument, regarding you as being perfect in Christ Jesus. That, again, is the meaning of the text, and the same meaning, only a different phase of it.

The last meaning is that the sacrifices of the Jews did not give believing Jews peace of mind for any length of time; they had to come again and again and again, because they felt that those sacrifices did not give them a perfect justification before God. But, behold, beloved, you and I are complete in Jesus (Col. 2:10). We have no need for any other sacrifice. All others we disclaim. "He hath perfected [us] for ever" (Heb. 10:14). We may set our consciences at ease, because we are truly, really, and everlastingly accepted in Him. "He hath perfected for ever them that are sanctified" (v. 14).

Now, what is left, except to ask you, "Are you a sanctified person?" I have known a man to say sometimes to a believer, "Well, you look so sanctified. Ah! You must be one of those sanctified people!" Well, if they said that to me, I would reply, "I wish you would prove it, then." What can be more holy than to be a sanctified man?

Let me ask you, then, "Are you sanctified?" You may say, "I feel so sinful." But I do not ask you that. Rather, I ask you whether you are set apart to God's service. Can you say,

> Dear Lord, I give myself away,
> 'Tis all that I can do?

Can you say, "Take me just as I am, and make use of me; I desire to be wholly thine"? Do you feel that for you to live is Christ (Phil. 1:21); that there is not any reason for which you are living except for Christ; that Christ is the great aim of your ambition, the great objective of all your labors; that you are like Samson, a

Nazarite, consecrated to God? Oh, then, remember that you are perfected in Christ (Heb. 10:14).

But, dear reader, if you are not sanctified to God in this sense—if you live unto yourself, unto pleasure, and unto the world—then you are not perfected in Christ. And what will become of you? God will give you no access to Him. God will not use you in His service; you will have no rest in your conscience; and in the day when God will come to separate the precious from the vile, He will say, "Those are My precious ones, who have the blood on them. But these have rejected Christ; they have lived unto themselves; they were dead while they lived, and they are damned now that they are dead."

Take heed of that! May God give you grace to be sanctified to God, and then you will be forever perfected through Christ.

Chapter Two

Threefold Sanctification

Sanctified by God the Father.
—Jude 1:1

Sanctified in Christ Jesus.
—1 Corinthians 1:2

Through sanctification of the Spirit.
—1 Peter 1:2

As we study the Scriptures, we come to recognize the union of the three divine persons of the Trinity, in all their gracious and glorious acts. Although we rejoice to recognize each person of the Trinity, they are always most distinctly a Trinity in unity. We believe in one God, and our watchword still remains—"Hear, O Israel: the LORD our God is one LORD" (Deut. 6:4).

31

Many young believers talk very unwisely when they claim to have preferences in the persons of the Trinity. They think of Christ as if He were the embodiment of everything that is lovely and gracious, while the Father they regard as severely just, but destitute of kindness. And how foolish are those who magnify the decree of the Father, or the atonement of the Son, thereby depreciating the work of the Spirit! In deeds of grace, not one of the three persons of the Trinity acts apart from the rest. They are as united in their deeds as they are in their essence. In their love toward the chosen, they are one; and in the actions that flow from that great central source, they are still undivided.

I want you to notice this in the case of sanctification. While we may, without the slightest mistake, speak of sanctification as the work of the Spirit, yet we must take heed that we do not view it as if the Father and the Son had no part in it. It is correct to speak of sanctification as the work of the Father, of the Spirit, and of the Son. God still says, "Let *us* make man in our image, after our likeness" (Gen. 1:26, italics added), and thus we are

> ***his*** *workmanship, created in Christ Jesus unto good works, which God hath before ordained that we should walk in them.* (Eph. 2:10, emphasis added)

32

Dear reader, I beg you to notice and carefully consider the value that God sets upon real holiness, since the three persons are represented as coworking to produce a church without "spot, or wrinkle, or any such thing" (Eph. 5:27). Those men who despise holiness of heart are in direct conflict with God. Holiness is the architectural plan upon which God builds up His living temple. (See 1 Peter 2:5.)

We read in Scripture of the "beauties of holiness" (Ps. 110:3); nothing is beautiful before God except that which is holy. All the glory of Lucifer, that "son of the morning" (Isa. 14:12), could not screen him from divine abhorrence when he had defiled himself by sin. "Holy, holy, holy" (Rev. 4:8), the continual cry of the cherubim, is the loftiest song that that creature can offer, and the noblest that the Divine Being can accept.

Notice that God considers holiness to be His choice treasure. It is like the seal upon His heart (Song 8:6), and like the signet upon His right hand (Jer. 22:24). He could as soon cease to exist as cease to be holy, and sooner renounce the sovereignty of the world than tolerate anything in His presence contrary to purity, righteousness, and holiness.

You who profess to be followers of Christ, I pray that you will set a high value upon purity of life and godliness of conversation. Consider the blood of Christ as the foundation of your hope, but never speak disparagingly of the work of the Spirit, which makes you fit for "the inheritance of the saints in light" (Col. 1:12). Yes, prize it; prize it so heartily that you dread the very appearance of evil. Prize it so that, in your most ordinary actions, you may be

> *a royal priesthood, an holy nation, a peculiar people; that ye should show forth the praises of him who hath called you out of darkness into his marvellous light.* *(1 Pet. 2:9)*

At first, I intended to use the word *sanctification* in the way in which it is understood among theologians; for you must know that the term *sanctification* has a far narrower meaning in schools of theology than it has in Scripture. I decided, however, that I want you to notice that sanctification is treated in Scripture in various ways. It may in some way illuminate the understanding of many believers, if I simply draw attention not to the theological, but to the scriptural, uses of the term *sanctification*, and show that, in God's Holy Word, it has a much wider meaning than is agreed upon by systematic theologians.

It has been well said that the Book of God, like the works of God, is not systematically arranged. How different is the freedom of nature from the orderly precision of the scientific museum! If you were to visit the British Museum, you would see all the animals there, placed in cases according to their respective classifications. On the other hand, you go into God's world and find dog and sheep, horse and cow, lion and vulture, elephant and ostrich, all roaming abroad as if no zoology had ever ventured to arrange them in classes. The various rocks are not laid in the order in which the geologist draws them in his books, nor are the stars marked off in the sky according to their sizes.

The order of nature is variety. Science simply arranges and classifies, in order to assist the memory. In the same manner, systematic theologians, when they come to deal with God's Word, find scriptural truths arranged, not in order for the classroom, but for common life. The theologian is as useful as the analytical chemist, or the anatomist, but still, the Bible is not arranged as a body of theology. It is a handbook to heaven; it is a guide to eternity, meant for the man at the plow as much as for the scholar at his table. It is a primer for babes, as well as a classic for sages. It is the humble, uneducated man's book; and though there are depths in it, in which the elephant may swim, there are shallows where the lamb may wade. We bless God that He has not given us a body of theology in which we might lose ourselves, but that He has given us His own Word, put into the very best practical form for our daily use and edification.

Set Apart unto God

It is a recognized truth among us, that the Old Testament very often helps us to understand the New, while the New also expounds the Old. With God's Word, self-interpretation is the best. "Diamond cuts diamond" is a rule with jewelers; so must it be with students of Scripture. Those who wish to know best God's Word, must study it in its own light.

Now, in the Old Testament we find the word *sanctify* very frequently indeed, and it is used there in three senses. Let me call your attention to the first one.

The word *sanctify* in the Old Testament frequently has the meaning of "setting apart." It signifies the taking of something that was common before, that might legitimately have been put to ordinary uses, and setting it apart for God's service alone. It was then called sanctified or holy.

Take, for instance, the passage in Exodus 13:2: "Sanctify unto me all the firstborn." On account of the destruction of the firstborn of Egypt, God claimed the firstborn of men and the firstborn of cattle to be His. Members of the tribe of Levi were set apart to be the representatives of the firstborn, to stand before the Lord to minister day and night in His tabernacle and in His temple. Those who were set apart to be priests and Levites were, as a result, said to be sanctified.

There is an earlier use of the term *sanctified* in Genesis 2:3:

> *And God blessed the seventh day, and sanctified it: because that in it he had rested from all his work which God created and made.*

The seventh day had been an ordinary portion of time before, but He set it apart for His own service, that on the seventh day man should do no work for himself, but rest and serve his Maker. That is why, in Leviticus 27:14, you read, "And when a man shall sanctify his house to be holy unto the LORD," and so on. This particular verse was meant as a direction to devout Jews who set apart a field or house to be God's, intending that either the produce of the field or the occupation of the house should be wholly given either to God's priests or to the Levites, or that, in some other way, it should be set apart for holy uses. Now, nothing was done to the house; there were no ceremonies; we do not read that it was cleansed or washed or sprinkled with blood; but the mere fact that it was set apart for God was considered to be a sanctification.

Likewise, in Exodus 29:44, we read that God said, "I will sanctify the tabernacle of the congregation, and the altar," by which, plainly enough, He meant that He would set it apart to be His house, the special place of His abode, where, between the wings of the cherubim, the bright light of the Shekinah might shine forth—the glorious evidence that the Lord God dwelt in the midst of His people.

The following verses are to the same effect:

◇ The sanctification of the altar, instruments, and vessels, in Numbers 7:1

◇ The setting apart of Eleazer, the son of Abinadab, to keep the ark of the Lord while it was at Kirjathjearim, in 1 Samuel 7:1

◇ The establishment of cities of refuge, in
   Joshua 20:7, where we find in the original
   manuscripts that the word rendered
   "appointed" is the same that elsewhere is
   translated "sanctified"

It is clear from the Old Testament that the
word *sanctify* sometimes has the meaning simply and only of "setting apart for holy uses."
   This explains the text in John 10:36,
which reads,

> *Say ye of him, whom the Father hath*
> *sanctified, and sent into the world, Thou*
> *blasphemest; because I said, I am the*
> *Son of God?*

Jesus Christ here speaks of Himself as having
been "sanctified" by His Father. Now, He was
not purged from sin, for He had no sin in Him.
Immaculately conceived, and gloriously preserved from all touch or stain of evil, He
needed no sanctifying work of the Spirit within
Him to purge Him from dross or corruption.
All that is here intended is that He was set
apart.
   Likewise, in that notable and well-known
passage in John 17:19, He meant only that He
gave Himself up specially to God's service, to

be occupied only with His Father's business: "And for their sakes I sanctify myself, that they also might be sanctified through the truth." As a result, He could also say, "My meat is to do the will of him that sent me, and to finish his work" (John 4:34).

Dear friend, you now understand our first text, "Sanctified by God the Father" (Jude 1:1). Surely it means that God the Father has specially set apart or sanctified His people. This does not mean that God the Father actively works in the believer's heart, although Paul tells us "it is God which worketh in [us] both to will and to do" (Phil. 2:13)—that task belongs directly and effectively to the Holy Spirit—but that He, in the decree of election, separated unto Himself a people who were to be sanctified to Himself forever and ever. By the gift of His Son for them, He redeemed them from among men, that they might be holy; and, by continually sending forth the Spirit, He fulfills His divine purpose that they should be a separate people, sanctified from all the rest of mankind.

In this sense, every Christian is perfectly sanctified already. We may speak of believers as those who are sanctified by God the Father; that is to say, they are set apart. They were set apart before they were created; they were legally set apart by the purchase of Christ; they are manifestly and visibly set apart by the effectual calling of the Spirit of grace. They are, in this sense, at all times sanctified; and, speaking of the work as it concerns God the Father, they are completely sanctified unto the Lord forever.

Is this doctrine not clear enough to you? Then leave the doctrine for a moment, and look at it practically. Dear readers, have we ever realized this truth as we ought to? When a vessel, cup, altar, or instrument was set apart for divine worship, it was never used for common purposes again. No man except the priest could drink out of the golden cup; the altar could not be trifled with; God's bronze laver was not for ordinary ablution;[1] even the tongs upon the altar and the snuffers for the lamps were never to be profaned for any common purpose whatsoever.

What a solemn and meaningful fact this is! If you and I are, indeed, sanctified by God the Father, we should never be used for any purpose but for God. "What," you say, "not for ourselves?" No, not for ourselves. "Ye are not your own...ye are bought with a price" (1 Cor.

---

[1]Laver: a large basin used for ceremonial ablutions, or washings, in the ancient Jewish tabernacle and temple worship.

6:19–20). "But," you say again, "must we not work and earn our own bread?" Truly, you must, but not with that as your chief purpose. You must still be diligent "in business; fervent in spirit; serving the Lord" (Rom. 12:11). And, if you are servants, you are to serve "not with eyeservice, as menpleasers; but as the servants of Christ" (Eph. 6:6).

If you think you can say, "I have an occupation in which I cannot serve the Lord," then leave it; you have no right in it. I think there is no calling—certainly no lawful calling—in which man can be found, in which he may not be able to say, "Whether I eat or drink, or whatsoever I do, I do all to the glory of God." (See 1 Corinthians 10:31.) The Christian is no more a common man than the altar was a common place. It is as great a sacrilege for the believer to live unto himself, or to live unto the world, as if you and I had profaned the Most Holy Place, used the holy fire for our own kitchen, the censer for a common perfume, or the candlestick for our own bedroom. These things were God's; no one could venture to make use of them without the right to do so. And we are God's and must be used only for Him.

Oh, Christians, if only you would know this, and know it fully! You are Christ's men and women, God's men and women, servants of God through Jesus Christ. You are not to do your own works; you are not to live for your own objectives. You are to say at all times, "God forbid that I should glory, save in the cross of our Lord Jesus Christ" (Gal. 6:14). You are to take for your motto, "For to me to live is Christ, and to die is gain" (Phil. 1:21).

Sometimes I fear that nine out of ten professing Christians have never recognized this fact. They think that if they were to devote a part of their possessions, a part of themselves, or a part of their time, that would be enough. Oh, but Christ did not buy a part of you! He bought you entire—body, soul, and spirit—and He must have you, the whole man. Oh, if you are to be saved partly by Him and partly by yourselves, then live to yourselves; but if God has wholly set you apart to be vessels of mercy (see Romans 9:23) fitted for His use, oh, do not rob the Lord; do not treat as common cups those things that are as the bowls of the altar.

There is another practical thought to be considered here. It was a crime that brought destruction upon Babylon when Belshazzar, in his drunken frolic, cried, "Bring forth the cups of the Lord, the goodly spoil of the temple at Jerusalem." (See Daniel 5:2–3.) They brought the golden candlestick, and there it stood, flaming high in the midst of the marble hall. The despot, surrounded by his wives and his concubines, filled high the bowl with the foaming drink. He then commanded them to pass around the cups of Jehovah, and the heathen and the worshippers of idols drank confusion to the God of heaven and earth.

In that moment, just as the sacred vessel touched the sacrilegious lip, a hand was seen mysteriously writing out his doom: "Thou art weighed in the balances, and art found wanting" (Dan. 5:27). This was the crime that filled up the ephah of his sin.[2] The measure of his iniquity was fully accomplished. He had used, for lascivious and drunken purposes, vessels that belonged to Jehovah, the God of the whole earth.

Oh, take heed, take heed, you who profess to be sanctified by the blood of the covenant, that you do not consider the covenant an unholy thing. See to it that you do not make your bodies, which you profess to be set apart for God's service, slaves of sin (see Romans 6:6), or "your members servants...[of] iniquity unto iniquity" (Rom. 6:19)—lest you should hear in that hour the voice of the recording angel as he

---

[2]Ephah: an ancient Hebrew unit of dry measure equal to about .65 of a bushel.

cries, "Thou art weighed in the balances and found wanting."

"Be ye clean, that bear the vessels of the LORD" (Isa. 52:11). And you who hope that you are Christ's, and have a humble faith in Him each morning, see that you walk circumspectly (Eph. 5:15), that by no means you prostitute, to the service of sin, that which was set apart in the eternal covenant of grace to be God's alone. If you and I are tempted to sin, we must reply, "No, let another man do that, but I cannot. I am God's man; I am set apart for Him. 'How then can I do this great wickedness, and sin against God?' (Gen. 39:9)." Let dedication enforce sanctification.

Think of the dignity to which God has called you—Jehovah's vessels, set apart for the Master's use. May everything that would make you impure, be far, far away. When Antiochus Epiphanes offered a sow on the altar of the Lord in the temple at Jerusalem, his awful death might have been easily foretold.[3] Oh, how many there are who profess to be sanctified servants of the Lord, who have offered unclean flesh upon the altar of God, who have made religion a stalking-horse to their own advantage, and who

---

[3] Antiochus Epiphanes: ruler of Syria and the Seleucid Dynasty from 175 to 164 B.C. See Appendix A.

have adopted the faith in order to gain respect and applause among men!

What does the Lord say concerning such things? "Vengeance belongeth unto me, I will recompense, saith the Lord" (Heb. 10:30). For many, their god is their stomach; they glory in their shame; they mind earthly things; and they die justly accursed. (See Philippians 3:19.) They are spots in your solemn feasts (Jude 1:12), "wandering stars, to whom is reserved the blackness of darkness for ever" (v. 13). But you, beloved, do not become carried away with the error of the wicked (2 Pet. 3:17), but keep yourselves "unspotted from the world" (James 1:27).

Declared and Regarded as Holy

Secondly, in the Old Testament, the word *sanctify* is sometimes used in another sense— one that I do not think is hinted at in our biblical encyclopedias, but that is needed to make the subject complete. The word *sanctify* is used, not only to signify that the thing is set apart for holy uses, but also that it is to be *regarded, treated, and declared as a holy thing*. I will give you an example from Isaiah 8:13.

In this passage we read, "Sanctify the LORD of hosts himself." You may clearly understand that the Lord does not need to be set apart for holy uses; the Lord of Hosts does not need to be purified, for He is holiness itself. However, what the sense of the word actually means is that we are to adore and reverence the Lord; with fear and trembling we must approach His throne and regard Him as the Holy One of Israel. Let me give you other instances of this.

When Nadab and Abihu, as recorded in Leviticus 10, offered a sacrifice to God and put strange fire on the altar, the fire of the Lord went forth and consumed them, and this was the reason given: "I will be sanctified in them that come nigh me" (Lev. 10:3). By this He did not mean that He would be set apart, nor that He would be made holy by purification, but that He would be treated and regarded as a Most Holy Being, with whom such liberties were not to be taken.

Another example is found in Numbers 20, on that unfortunate occasion when Moses lost his temper and smote the rock twice, saying, "Hear now, ye rebels; must we fetch you water out of this rock?" (Num. 20:10). Then the Lord said that Moses would see the Promised Land, but would never enter it, the reason being, "Because ye believed me not, to sanctify me in the eyes of the children of Israel" (v. 12). By this He meant that Moses had not acted so as to honor God's name among the people.

An even more familiar instance occurs in what is commonly called the Lord's Prayer: "Our Father which art in heaven, Hallowed be thy name" (Matt. 6:9). The word *hallowed* is simply an English variation of *sanctified*, because the Greek reads, "Sanctified be thy name." Now, we know that God's name does not need purifying or setting apart, so the sense here can only be "Let thy name be reverenced and adored throughout the whole earth, and let men regard it as being a sacred and holy thing."

Beloved, do we not have some light here concerning our second text, "Sanctified in Christ Jesus" (1 Cor. 1:2)? If the word *sanctified* may mean "regarded as holy and treated as such," can you not see how in Christ Jesus the saints are regarded by God as being holy, and are treated as such? Surely, we do not lay that down as being the only meaning of the text, for another sense may yet be attached to it.

There have been certain believers who have elaborated on our being sanctified in Christ, and have almost forgotten the work of the Spirit. Now, if they only speak of our being sanctified in Christ, in the sense of being treated as holy (or, in fact, as being justified), we have no quarrel with them; but if they deny the work of the Spirit, they are guilty of deadly error.

I have sometimes heard the term *imputed sanctification* used, which is sheer absurdity. One cannot use the term *imputed justification* and be at all correct. *Imputed righteousness* is correct enough and implies a glorious doctrine, but justification is neither imputed nor attributed; it is actually conferred, or given. We are justified through the imputed righteousness of Christ, but as to being "imputedly sanctified," no one who understands the use of language can speak this way. The term is inaccurate and unscriptural.

I know it is said that the Lord Jesus is made "of God...unto us wisdom, and righteousness, and sanctification, and redemption" (1 Cor. 1:30), but this sanctification is not by imputation, nor does the text say so. Why, you might as readily prove imputed wisdom or imputed redemption by this text, as force it to teach imputed sanctification.

It is a fact that for the sake of what Jesus Christ did, God's people—though in themselves they are only partially sanctified because they are yet subject to sin—are for Christ's sake treated and regarded as if they are perfectly holy. But this, according to theological definitions, is justification rather than sanctification, although it must be admitted that the Scripture sometimes uses the word *sanctification* in such a manner so as to make it tantamount to justification. By this, however, we can clearly see that God's people have access with boldness to the Lord (see Hebrews 4:16), because they are regarded, through Christ, as though they are perfectly holy.

Oh, Christian, think about this for a moment! A holy God cannot have dealings with unholy men. A holy God—and is not Christ Jesus God?—cannot have communion with unholiness, and yet you and I are unholy. How, then, does Christ receive us to His bosom? How does His Father walk with us and find Himself yielding His consent? Because He views us, not in ourselves, but in our great covenantal Head, the Second Adam. He looks at us,

> Not as we were in Adam's fall,
> When sin and ruin covered all;
> But as we'll stand another day,
> Fairer than sun's meridian ray.

He looks on the deeds of Christ as ours, on His perfect obedience and sinless life as ours, and thus we may sing in the language of Hart—

> With thy spotless garments on,
> Holy as the Holy One.

We may boldly enter into that which is within the veil, where no unholy thing may come, yet where we may venture because God views us as holy in Christ Jesus.

This is a great and precious doctrine; yet the use of the term *sanctification* in any other sense than that in which it is commonly employed, as meaning "the work of the Spirit," tends to foster confused ideas, and really does, I fear, lead some to despise the work of the Spirit of God. I think it is better, in ordinary conversation between Christians, to speak of sanctification without confusing it with what is quite a distinctly different act, namely, justification through the imputed righteousness of our Lord and Savior Jesus Christ. Yet, if we hear a brother talk in this manner, we must not be too severe with him, as though he had certainly strayed from the faith, for in Scripture, the terms *sanctification* and *justification* are frequently used interchangeably, and Christ's righteousness made the subject matter of both works of grace.

Purified and Made Holy

We now come to the usual sense in which the word *sanctification* is employed. It means actually "to purify or make holy," not merely to set apart or to account holy, but to make really and actually so in nature. You have the word in this sense in many places in the Old Testament. Let us examine it in Exodus 19:10–12.

On the third day of the third month, God was about to proclaim His holy Law on top of Mount Sinai, and the mandate went forth, "Sanctify [the people] to day and to morrow" (v. 10). This sanctification consisted of certain outward deeds by which their bodies and clothes were put into a state of cleanliness and their souls were brought into a reverential state of awe.

Likewise, in the third chapter of Joshua, you find, when the children of Israel were about to cross the Jordan, it was said, "Sanctify yourselves: for tomorrow the LORD will do wonders among you" (v. 5). They were to prepare themselves to be beholders of a scene so grand: when the Jordan was driven back and the river was utterly dried up before the feet of the priests of God. There was, in this case, an actual purification. Men in the old times were sprinkled with blood, and they were thus sanctified from defilement and considered to be pure in the sight of God. This is the sense in which we view our third text, "Through sanctification of the Spirit" (1 Pet.

1:2), and this, I repeat, is the general sense in which we understand it in common conversation among Christians.

Sanctification begins in regeneration. The Spirit of God infuses into man the new element called the spirit, which is a third and higher nature, so that the believing man becomes body, soul, *and spirit*. In this he is distinct and distinguished from all other men of the race of Adam. This work, which begins in regeneration, is carried on in two ways: by vivification and by mortification; that is, by giving life to that which is good, and by sending death to that which is evil in the man.

Mortification is the process whereby the lusts of the flesh are subdued and kept under; and vivification, the process by which the life that God has put within us, is made to be "a well of water springing up into everlasting life" (John 4:14). This is carried on every day in what we call perseverance, by which the Christian is preserved and continued in a gracious state, and is made to abound in good works (see 2 Corinthians 9:8) unto the praise and glory of God. And it culminates, or comes to perfection, in glory, when the soul, being thoroughly purged, is caught up to dwell with holy beings (see 1 Thessalonians 4:17) at "the right hand of the Majesty on high" (Heb. 1:3).

Now, this work, though we commonly speak of it as being the work of the Spirit, is quite as much the work of the Lord Jesus Christ as of the Spirit. In looking for texts on the subject, I have been struck with the fact that where I found one verse speaking of it as the Spirit's work, I found another in which it was treated as the work of Jesus Christ. I can well understand that my second text, "Sanctified in Christ Jesus" (1 Cor. 1:2), has as great a fullness of meaning as the third, "Through sanctification of the Spirit" (1 Pet. 1:2). Oh, that you may yet know how precious to a believer is the purifying work of sanctification!

Sanctification is a work *in* us, not a work *for* us. It is a work in us, and there are two agents: one is the worker who works this sanctification effectually—that is the Spirit; and the other, the efficacious means by which the Spirit works this sanctification—Jesus Christ and His most precious blood.

Imagine, to put it as plainly as we can, there is a garment that needs to be washed. There is a person to wash it, and there is a bath in which it is to be washed. In terms of sanctification, the person is the Holy Spirit, but the bath is the precious blood of Christ. It is entirely correct to speak of the person cleansing as being the sanctifier. It is quite as

54

accurate to speak of that which is in the bath and which makes the garment clean, as being the sanctifier, too. So, the Spirit of God sanctifies us; He works it effectively; but He sanctifies us through the blood of Christ, through the water that flowed with the blood from Christ's side.

I repeat my illustration: imagine a garment that is black. A fuller,[4] in order to make the garment white, uses nitre and soap;[5] and both the fuller and the soap are cleansers. Likewise, both the Holy Spirit and the atonement of Christ are sanctifiers. This should be enough of an explanation of my point. Now, let us look further into this doctrine.

The Spirit of God is the great worker by whom we are cleansed. I will not cite the texts here. Perhaps you have read the Baptist Confession of Faith[6] and the Catechism.[7] They will

---

[4]Fuller: one who shrinks and thickens cloth (especially woolen cloth) by moistening, heating, and pressing.

[5]Nitre: also known as *niter*, is an oxidizing agent that is often white, gray, or colorless.

[6]The Baptist Confession of Faith: adopted by the Ministers and Messengers of the general assembly that met in London in 1689. See Appendix B.

[7]Catechism: Many evangelical churches of Spurgeon's time copied some of the teaching methods of the High Church. The basic doctrinal beliefs of the church were written as small books and then taught in Sunday school classes, instead of catechism classes.

furnish you with an abundance of texts on this
subject, for this is a doctrine that is generally
accepted—that it is the Spirit of God who cre-
ates in us a new heart and a right spirit, according to the whole tone of the covenant:

> *A new heart also will I give you, and a*
> [right] *spirit will I put within*
> *you....And I will put my spirit within*
> *you, and cause you to walk in my stat-*
> *utes.* (Ezek. 36:26–27)

The Spirit renews and changes the nature,
turns the bias of the will, and makes us seek
that which is good and right, so that every
good thing in us may be described as "the fruit
of the Spirit" (Gal. 5:22), and all our virtues
and all our graces are efficiently worked in us
by the Spirit of the living God. Never, never,
never forget this. Oh, it will be an evil day for
any church when the members begin to think
lightly of the work of the Holy Spirit within us!
We delight to magnify the work of Christ *for*
us, but we must not depreciate the work of the
blessed Spirit *in* us.

In the days of my venerable predecessor,
Dr. Gill, who was fully of the opinion of ul-
tra-Calvinists, this vicious evil broke out in the
Metropolitan Tabernacle. There were some

who believed in "imputed sanctification," and denied the work of the blessed Spirit. Recently, I read a note written in our old church book, in the doctor's own handwriting, concerning the deliberate opinion of the church in those days. It went as follows:

Agreed: That to deny the internal sanctification of the Spirit, as a principle of grace and holiness wrought in the heart, or as consisting of grace communicated to and implanted in the soul, which, though but a begun work, and as yet incomplete, is an abiding work of grace, and will abide, notwithstanding all corruptions, temptations, and snares, and be performed by the Author of it until the Day of Christ, when it will be the saints' meetness [fitness] for eternal glory; is a grievous error, which highly reflects dishonor on the blessed Spirit and His operations of grace on the heart, is subversive of true religion and powerful godliness, and renders persons unfit for church communion. Wherefore, it is further agreed, that such persons who appear to have embraced this error be not admitted to the communion of this church, and should any such who are members of it appear to have received it and continued in it, that they be forthwith excluded from it.

Two members, who were then present, declared themselves to be of the opinion condemned in the above resolution; and a third person, who was absent, was well known to have been under this awful delusion. All three of them were consequently excluded, that very evening, from fellowship. In addition, a person of another church, who held the opinion thus condemned, was forbidden to receive Communion. His pastor at Kettering was written to upon the subject, and was warned not to allow so great an errorist to remain in fellowship. Dr. Gill thought the error to be so deadly, that he used the pruning knife at once; he did not stop until it spread, but he cut off the very twigs.

This is one of the benefits of church discipline, when we are enabled to carry it out under God: that it does destroy the growth of error in its very early stages, and that through such discipline, those who are not infected as yet, are kept from it by the blessed providence of God through the instrumentality of the church. I have always believed, and still believe and teach, that the work of the Spirit in us, whereby we are conformed unto Christ's image, is as absolutely necessary for our salvation as is the work of Jesus Christ, by which He cleanses us from our sins.

Pause here for a moment, but do not allow me to distract you from the substance of this chapter. While the Spirit of God is said in Scripture to be the Author of sanctification, yet there is a visible agent that must not be forgotten. "Sanctify them," said Christ, "through thy truth: thy word is truth" (John 17:17).

Look up all the passages of Scripture that prove that the instrument of our sanctification is the Word of God. You will find that there are very many. It is the Word of God that sanctifies the soul. The Spirit of God brings to our minds the commands and precepts and doctrines of truth (see John 14:26), and applies them with power. These are heard in the ear, and, being received in the heart, they work in us to will and to do of God's good pleasure (Phil. 2:13). How important, then, that the truth should be preached! How necessary that you never tolerate a ministry that leaves out the great doctrines or the great precepts of the Gospel! The truth is the sanctifier, and if we do not hear the truth, we will certainly not grow in sanctification.

We only progress in sound living as we progress in sound understanding. "Thy word is a lamp unto my feet, and a light unto my path" (Ps. 119:105). Do not say of such-and-such an error, "Oh, it is merely a matter of opinion," for if it is a mere matter of opinion today, it will be a matter of practice tomorrow. No man commits an error in judgment, without sooner or later committing an error in practice. Every grain of truth is like a grain of diamond dust; you would do well to prize it all.

> *Therefore, brethren, stand fast, and hold the traditions which ye have been taught, whether by word, or our epistle.*
> *(2 Thess. 2:15)*

"Hold fast the form of sound words" (2 Tim. 1:13), and in this day when doctrines are ridiculed, when creeds are despised, hold fast to that which you have received, that you may be found faithful among the faithless. For by so holding the truth, you will be sanctified by the Spirit of God. The agent, then, is the Spirit of God working through the truth.

But, now, let me bring you back to the substance of this matter. We are sanctified, in another sense, through Christ Jesus, because it is His blood—and the water that flowed from His side—in which the Spirit washes our hearts from the defilement of and the tendency toward sin. It is said of our Lord,

> *Christ also loved the church, and gave himself for it; that he might sanctify and*

cleanse it with the washing of water by the word, that he might present it to himself a glorious church, not having spot, or wrinkle, or any such thing.

(Eph. 5:25–27)

There are hundreds of texts of this kind. Remember these verses:

Jesus also, that he might sanctify the people with his own blood, suffered without the gate. *(Heb. 13:12)*

He that sanctifieth and they who are sanctified are all of one: for which cause he is not ashamed to call them brethren. *(Heb. 2:11)*

Thou shalt call his name JESUS: for he shall save his people from their sins. *(Matt. 1:21)*

God forbid that I should glory, save in the cross of our Lord Jesus Christ, by whom the world is crucified unto me, and I unto the world. *(Gal. 6:14)*

In that memorable passage where Paul, struggling with corruption, exclaimed, "O wretched man that I am! who shall deliver me from the body of this death?" (Rom. 7:24), the answer does not concern the Holy Spirit, but he said, "I thank God through Jesus Christ our Lord" (v. 25). I do not have room enough here to write all the texts that would apply, but there are many passages to the effect that our sanctification is the work of Jesus Christ. He is our sanctifier, for He filled the sacred laver of regeneration in which we are washed, filled it with the blood and with the water that flowed from His side, and in this we are washed by the Holy Spirit.

There is no sanctification through the law, for the Spirit does not use legal precepts to sanctify us. There is no purification by mere dictates of morality, for the Spirit of God does not use them, either. No, for just as when Marah's waters were bitter (Exod. 15:23), Moses, in order to make them sweet, commanded the people to take a tree and cast it into the waters, and they were sweet (v. 25), so the Spirit of God, finding our natures bitter, takes the tree of Calvary, casts it into the stream, and makes everything pure. He finds us lepers, and to make us clean, He dips the hyssop of faith into the precious blood and sprinkles it upon us, and we are clean. (See Leviticus 12:5–7.)

There is a mysterious efficacy in the blood of Christ, not merely to make satisfaction for sin, but to bring about the death of sin. The blood appears before God, and He is well pleased. It falls on us: lusts wither, and old corruptions feel the death stroke. Dagon falls before the ark of the Lord (see 1 Samuel 5:2–3), and although its stump is left (v. 4) and corruptions still remain, Christ will put an end to all our inbred sins, and through Him we will mount to heaven, "perfect, even as [our] Father which is in heaven is perfect" (Matt. 5:48).

Just as the Spirit only works through the truth, so the blood of Christ only works through faith. Again I say, turn to your Bibles at your leisure, and find the many passages that speak of faith as sanctifying the soul and purifying the mind. Our faith lays hold of the precious atonement of Christ. It sees Jesus suffering on the tree, and it says, "I vow revenge against the sins that nailed Him there." His precious blood works in us an extreme contempt for all sin; and the Spirit, through the truth, working by faith, applies the precious blood of sprinkling, and we are made clean, and are "accepted in the beloved" (Eph. 1:6).

I am afraid that I have confused and obscured this matter with words. Even so, I think I may have suggested some trains of thought that will lead you to see that Holy Scripture teaches us a sanctification that is not narrow and concise, so as to be written down with a short definition, as in our creed books, but wide, large, and expansive—a work in which we are sanctified by God the Father, sanctified in Christ Jesus, and yet have our sanctification through the Spirit of God. Oh, my dear readers, strive after practical holiness! You who love Christ, do not let anyone say of you, "There is a Christian, but he is worse than other men." It is not our eloquence, our learning, our fame, or our wealth, that can ever commend Christ to the world; it is only the holy living of Christians.

Just the other day, I was talking with a fellow minister about a current movement that I fear will be an immense injury to Christ's church. I said that I feared, lest it should be made an opportunity for strife among believers; error must be corrected, but love must not be wounded. He remarked—and I thought it was so truthful—that the only way by which the dissent from the established church flourished in earlier times, was by the then superior holiness of the dissenting ministers. It would often happen that, while the clergyman of the established church was off hunting, the dissenting minister would visit the sick. And then he said, "If our ministers become political and worldly, it will be all over with us. This is the way in which we will lose power."

I have never avoided rebuke, when I thought it necessary, but I hate contention. The only allowable strife is to see who can be the most holy, the most earnest, the most zealous; who can do the most for the poor and the ignorant; and who can lift Christ's Cross the highest. This is the way to lift up the members of any denomination—by the members of that body being more devout, more sanctified, more spiritually minded than the others. All infighting will only create strife and animosities and bickerings, and is not of the Spirit of God; but to live unto God and to be devoted to Him—this is the strength of the church; this will give us the victory, God helping us, and all the praise will be to His name.

As for those of you who are not converted, and are unregenerate, I cannot write to you concerning sanctification. I have opened a door, but you cannot enter. Only, remember, if you cannot enter into this, you cannot enter into heaven, for

Those holy gates for ever bar,
Pollution, sin, and shame;
None shall obtain admission there,
But followers of the Lamb.

May it be your privilege to come humbly and confess your sin, to ask and find forgiveness; for then, but not until then, there is hope that you may be sanctified in the spirit of your mind. The Lord bless you for Jesus' sake. Amen.

Chapter Three

Perfect
Sanctification

*By the which will we are sanctified through
the offering of the body of Jesus Christ
once for all.*
—Hebrews 10:10

D ear friends, ever since the Lord has quickened us by His grace, we have begun to look into ourselves and to search our hearts to see our condition before God. As a result, many things that once caused us no disquietude, now create great anxiety in us. We thought that we were all right, and we felt it was enough to be as good as others were. We dreamed that, if we were not quite as good as we should be, we would certainly grow better, though we did not stop to inquire how or why. We took stock of our condition and concluded that we were "rich, and increased with goods, and [had] need of nothing" (Rev. 3:17).

Even so, a change has come over the spirit of the scene; the grace of God has made us thoughtful and careful. We dare not take things haphazardly now. We test and prove things, for we are very anxious not to be deceived. We look upon eternal realities as being of the utmost consequence, so we dare not take for granted that we are right about them. We are afraid of being presumptuous; we desire to be sincere. We hold an examination within our spirits, and we are so afraid that we may be partial (although we probably are so), that we ask the Lord to search us and try us, to "see if there be any wicked way" in us, that He may lead us out of such a way, into the way of everlasting (Ps. 139:23–24).

This is all very wise and very proper, and I would not for a moment try to take the people of God away from a proper measure of this state of heart. And yet, may it never be forgotten that, in the sight of God, we are different in some respects than we will ever see ourselves to be if we look through the glass of feeling and consciousness. There are other matters to be taken into consideration, matters that our anxiety may lead us to overlook, and that our inward search may cause us to forget.

Faith reveals to us another position for the people of God besides that which they occupy in themselves. Some call it an evangelical fiction, and the like; but, thank God, it is a blessed fact that, sinners as we are in ourselves, yet we are saints in God's sight; and sinful as we feel ourselves to be, yet we are washed, cleansed, and sanctified in Jesus Christ. Notwithstanding all that we mourn over, the very fact that we do mourn over it becomes evidence that we are no longer what we once were, and do not stand now where we once stood.

We have passed from death unto life (1 John 3:14). We have escaped from underneath the dominion of law and into the kingdom of grace. We have come from being under the curse, and we dwell in the region of blessing. We have believed "on him that justifieth the ungodly, [and our] faith is counted for right-eousness" (Rom. 4:5). Therefore, there is no condemnation for us, because we are in Christ Jesus our Lord, and we walk no longer after the flesh, but after the Spirit (Rom. 8:1). Think of the noble position into which the grace of God has lifted all believers—the condition of sanctification that is spoken of in the text—for by the will of God "we are sanctified through the offering of the body of Jesus Christ once for all" (Heb. 10:10).

In this chapter, I will point out, first, the nature of the eternal will; second, the effectual sacrifice by which that will has been carried out; and, third, the everlasting result accomplished by that will through the sacrifice of the body of Christ. May the Holy Spirit, who has revealed the grand doctrine of justification, enable you to understand it and to feel its comforting power.

The Eternal Will

By "the eternal will," I mean the will by which we are sanctified (Heb. 10:10). This will must, first of all, be viewed as the will ordained from all eternity by the Father.

Ordained by the Father

The eternal decree of the infinite Jehovah was that a people whom He chose should be sanctified and set apart unto Himself. (See Deuteronomy 7:6.) The will of Jehovah stands fast forever and ever; and we know that it is altogether unchangeable, and that it has no beginning. It is an eternal will; we have no vacillating Deity, no fickle God. He wills changes, but He never changes His will.

> *He is in one mind, and who can turn him? and what his soul desireth, even that he doeth.*   *(Job 23:13)*

The will of God is invincible as well as eternal. We are told in the epistle to the Ephesians that He "worketh all things after the counsel of his own will" (Eph. 1:11). Who can "stay his hand, or say unto him, What doest thou" (Dan. 4:35)? The good pleasure of His will is never defeated: there cannot be such a thing as a vanquished God. "My counsel shall stand, and I will do all my pleasure" (Isa. 46:10), says the Lord. In fact, the will of God is the motive force of all things. "He spake, and it was done; he commanded, and it stood fast" (Ps. 33:9). His Word is omnipotent because His will is behind it, and puts force into it.

"God said, Let there be light: and there was light" (Gen. 1:3), because He willed that there should be light. He commanded creatures to come forth, as numerous as the drops of dew, to inhabit the world that He had made; and they came forth, flying, leaping, swimming, in varied orders of life, because He created them by His own will. His will is the secret power that sustains the universe, threads the starry orbs, and holds them like a necklace of light about the neck of nature. His will is the alpha and the omega of all things.

It was according to this eternal, invincible will of God that He chose, created, and set apart a people that should show forth the glory and riches of His grace, a people that should bear the image of His only begotten Son, a people that should joyfully and willingly serve Him in His courts forever and ever, a people who should be His own sons and daughters, to whom He would say, "I will dwell in them, and walk in them; and I will be their God, and they shall be my people" (2 Cor. 6:16). Thus stood the eternal will from ages past.

> *For whom he did foreknow, he also did predestinate to be conformed to the image of his Son, that he might be the firstborn among many brethren.*
> *(Rom. 8:29)*

Even so, the people concerning whom this will was set forth were dead in sin, defiled with evil, polluted by transgression. The old Serpent's venom was in their veins. They were in a condition to be set apart for the curse, but not to be set apart for the service of the thrice-holy God. And the question was, "How, then, can the will of the Immutable Invincible ever be carried out? How will these rebels become absolved of sin? How will these fountains of filth become clear as crystal, pouring forth floods of living water and divine praise? How will these unsanctified and defiled ones become sanctified unto the service of God? It must be, but how will it happen?"

Then came the priests, with smoking censers, and with basins full of blood, steaming because it had just come fresh from the slaughtered victims; and they sprinkled this blood upon the Book and upon the people, upon the altar and upon the mercy seat, and upon all the hangings of the tabernacle, and upon all the ground on which the worshippers walked; for almost all things under the law were sanctified by blood. This blood of bulls and of goats was everywhere—fresh every morning and renewed every evening.

Still, God's will was not done; the chosen were not thus sanctified; and we know they were not, because it is written, "Sacrifice and offering thou wouldest not" (Heb. 10:5). His will was not fulfilled in such sacrifices; it was not His will that they should sanctify the people. They were inefficacious to accomplish such an end, for, as the Scriptures say, it "is not possible that the blood of bulls and of goats should take away sins" (v. 4). And so, if these offerings had been all there was, generations upon generations of the house of Aaron and of the priests of the tribe of Levi might have come and gone, and yet the will decreed by the eternal Father would not have been an accomplished fact.

Performed by the Son

Thus we come to our second point concerning the eternal will, which is that this will by which we are sanctified was performed by the ever blessed Son. It was the will of God the Father, but it was carried out by the divine Son when He came into the world. A body was prepared for Him; He entered into that body in a manner that we will not attempt to conceive of; and He was the incarnate God. This incarnate God, by offering His own blood, by laying down His own life, by bearing in His own body the curse, and by enduring in His own spirit the wrath, was able to carry out the purpose of the everlasting Father in the purging of His people, in the setting apart of His chosen, and in making them henceforth holy unto the Lord.

Do you not see what the will of the Father was—that He should have a people that should be sanctified unto Himself? But that will could not be carried out by the blood of bulls and of goats; it had to be achieved by "the offering of the body of Jesus Christ once for all" (Heb. 10:10). Our Lord Jesus Christ has done what the will of the Father required for its perfect achievement. This is our satisfaction.

We will not enter at this time into a detailed account of our Lord's active and passive obedience, by which He magnified the law and set apart His people. However, I hope that you will never fall into the error of dividing the work of Christ, as some do, and saying, "Here He made atonement for sin, and there He did not." In these modern times, some believers have invented fancy ways of saying the most trivial things—things that are not even worth the trouble of thinking about—and yet, like babes with a new rattle, they make noise with them all day long.

It is amusing how so many wise professors make grave points out of mere hairsplitting distinctions; and if we do not agree with them, they put on a show of haughtiness, pitying our ignorance and glorying in themselves as superior persons who have an insight into things that ordinary Christians cannot see. God save us from having eyes that are so sharp that we are able to spy out new occasions for argument, and fresh reasons for making men into offenders for their mere words. I believe in the life of Christ as well as in His death, and I believe that He stood for me before God as much when He walked the acres of Palestine as when He hung on the cross at Jerusalem.

You cannot divide and split Him in two and say, "Only in these cases is He an example, and only in these cases is He an atonement."

Instead, you must take the entire Christ, and look at Him from the very first as "the Lamb of God, which taketh away the sin of the world" (John 1:29). "Oh," they say, "but He made no atonement except in His death." This is surely an absurdity in language. Ask yourself, "When does a man die?" There is the minute in which the soul separates from the body; but all the time that a man may be described as dying, he is still alive, is he not?

A man does not suffer once he is actually dead. What we call the pangs of death are truly and accurately the pangs of life. Death does not suffer; it is the end of suffering. A man is still alive while he suffers; and if they say, "It is Christ's death that makes an atonement, and not His life," I reply that death, alone and by itself, makes no atonement. Death in its natural sense, and not in this modern, unnatural sense of severance from life, does make atonement; but it cannot be viewed apart from life by any unsophisticated mind. If they must have distinctions, we could certainly make enough distinctions to worry them, but we have nobler work to do.

To us, our Lord's death seems to be the consummation of His life, the finishing stroke of a work that His Father had given Him to do among the sons of men. We view Him as having come in a body prepared for Him, to do the will of God *once,* and that "once" lasted throughout His one life on earth. We will not, however, dwell on any moot point, but genuinely rejoice that whatever was needed to make God's people wholly sanctified unto God, Christ has carried it out. "By the which will we are sanctified through the offering of the body of Jesus Christ once" (Heb. 10:10).

"It is finished" (John 19:30). Does the divine law require, in order for us to be accepted, perfect submission to the will of the Lord? He has rendered it. Does it ask for complete obedience to its precepts? He has presented the same. Does the fulfilled will of the Lord call for abject suffering, a sweat of blood, pangs unknown, and death itself? Christ has presented it all, whatever that "all" may be. When God created, His Word carried forth all His will. Likewise, when God redeemed, His blessed and incarnate Word accomplished all His will.

Applied by the Spirit

Just as God looked on each day's work and said, "It is good" (see Genesis 1:4), so, as He looks upon each part of the work of His dear Son, He can say of it, "It is good." The Father joins in the verdict of His Son, that it is finished

(John 19:30): all the will of God for the sanctification of His people is accomplished.

Dear Christian, this work must be applied to us by the Holy Spirit. It is the Holy Spirit who brings us to know that Jesus Christ has sanctified us, or set us apart, and made us acceptable with God. It is the Holy Spirit who has given us the New Testament, and shed a light upon the Old. It is the Holy Spirit who speaks to us through the ministers of Christ when He blesses them to help us to our conversion. It is especially the Holy Spirit who takes away from us all hope of being sanctified before God by any means of our own, brings us to see our need of cleansing and reconciliation, and then takes of the things of Christ and reveals them to us. Not without the going forth of His sacred power are we made to take the place of separation and dedication, to which the Lord ordained us from eternity.

Thus it is by the will of the Father, carried out by the Son, and applied by the Holy Spirit, that the church of God is regarded as sanctified before God, and is acceptable to Him.

I will not dwell any longer on this point, because these great things are best written of with few words: they are subjects that are better to be meditated upon by quiet thought than exhibited in writing.

The Effectual Sacrifice

In the second place, I invite you to consider the effectual sacrifice by which the will of God, with regard to the sanctity of His people, has been carried out. "By the which will we are sanctified through the offering of *the body of Jesus Christ*" (Heb. 10:10, italics added). What does this mean?

The Incarnation of God as Man

First of all, this implies His incarnation, which, of course, includes His eternal deity. We can never forget that Jesus Christ is God. The church has given forth many a valiant confession to His deity; and woe be to her should she ever hesitate on that glorious truth! Yet, sometimes she has great need to earnestly insist upon His humanity. As you bow before your glorious Lord and adore Him with all the sanctified, remember that He whom you worship was truly and really a man.

The Gospel of His incarnation is not a spiritual idea, nor a metaphor, nor a myth. In very deed and truth, the God who made heaven and earth came down to earth and hung upon a woman's breast as an infant.

That child, as He grew in wisdom and stature (Luke 2:52), was as certainly God as He is at this moment in glory. He was as surely God when He was here hungering and suffering, sleeping, eating, and drinking, as He was God when He hung up the morning stars and kindled the lamps of night, or as He will be when sun and moon shall grow dim at "the brightness of His coming" (2 Thess. 2:8).

Jesus Christ, very God of very God, certainly did stoop to become such as we are, and He was made in the likeness of sinful flesh. This is a truth you undoubtedly know, but I want you to grasp it and realize it; for it will help you to trust Christ if you clearly understand that, divine as He is, He is bone of your bone and flesh of your flesh (see Genesis 2:23)—your kinsman, though He is the Son of God.

All this is implied in the text, because it speaks of the offering of the *body* of Christ. But why did the author of Hebrews speak especially of the body? I think he did this in order to show us the reality of that offering: His soul suffered, and His soul's sufferings were the soul of His sufferings; yet, to make it palpable to you, to record it as a sure historical fact, he mentioned that there was an offering of the body of Christ.

The Whole of Christ

I take it, however, that the word *body* means "the whole of Christ"—that there was an offering made of all of Christ, the body of Him, or that of which He was constituted. It is my solemn conviction that His deity coworked with His humanity in the wondrous passion by which He has sanctified His elect.

I am told that Deity cannot suffer. I am expected to subscribe to that because theologians say so. Well, if it is true, then I will content myself with believing that the deity of Christ helped the humanity of Christ, by strengthening it to suffer more than it could otherwise have endured.

Yet, I believe that Deity can suffer, unorthodox as that notion may seem to be. I cannot believe in a God who is insusceptible to pain. If He pities and sympathizes, surely He must have some sensibilities. Is He a God of iron? If He wills it, He can do anything, and therefore He can suffer if He pleases.

It is not possible for God to be made to suffer; that would be a ridiculous supposition. Yet, if He wills to do so, He is certainly capable of doing that as well as anything else, for all things are possible to Him (Matt. 19:26). I look upon our Lord Jesus as, in His very Godhead, stooping down to bear the weight of human sin and human misery, sustaining it because He was divine, and able to bear what otherwise would have been too great a load. Thus, the whole of Christ was made a sacrifice for sin. It was the offering, not of the spirit of Christ, but of the very body of Christ—the essence, substance, and most manifest reality and personality of Jesus Christ, the Son of the Most High.

A Complete Offering

And Christ was wholly offered. I do not know how to explain my own thought here; but in order to accomplish the will of God in sanctifying all His people, Christ must be the offering, and He must be wholly offered. There were certain sacrifices that were only presented to God in part, so far as the consumption by fire was concerned. A part was eaten by the priest or by the offerer, and in that sense it was not a whole burnt offering. In this there was much precious truth set forth, of which I will not write here; but as our sin offering, making expiation for guilt, our blessed Lord and Master gave Himself wholly for us, as an atoning sacrifice and offering for sin.

That word *Himself* sums up all you can conceive to be in and of the Christ of God; and the pangs and griefs that went through Him like a fire, did consume Him and everything that was in Him. He bore all that could be borne, stooped to the lowest place to which humility could come, descended to the utmost abyss to which a descent of self-denial could be made. He "made himself of no reputation" (Phil. 2:7); He emptied Himself of all honor and glory, and "was made in the likeness of men" (v. 7). He gave up Himself without reserve. He saved others, though He did not save Himself. (See Luke 23:35.)

He spares us in our chastisements, but Himself He did not spare. He says of Himself, in the twenty-second Psalm, "I am a worm, and no man; a reproach of men, and despised of the people" (v. 6). You do not know, you cannot imagine, how fully the sacrifice was made by Christ. It was not only a sacrifice of all of Himself, but a complete sacrifice of every part of Himself for us. The blaze of eternal wrath for human sin was focused upon His head! The anguish that must have been endured by Him who stood in the place of millions of sinners, to be judged of God and stricken in their stead, is altogether inconceivable.

He Himself was perfectly innocent, yet in His own person He offered up a sacrifice that could honor the divine justice on account of a myriad of sins of the sons of men. This was a work far beyond all human realization! You may let go of your reason and your imagination, and rise into the seventh heaven of sublime conception as with eagles' wings, but you can never reach the utmost height. Here is the sum of the matter: "Thanks be unto God for his unspeakable gift" (2 Cor. 9:15), for unspeakable and inconceivable it certainly is when we view the Lord Jesus as a sacrifice for the sins of men.

A Singular Offering

This offering was made once, *and only once.* The meaning of our text lies in the finishing words of it: "through the offering of the body of Jesus Christ once for all" (Heb. 10:10). Those words, *for all,* are very properly put in by the translators, but you must not make a mistake as to their meaning. The text does not mean that Christ offered Himself up once for *all*—that is, for all mankind. That may be a doctrine of Scripture, or it may not be a doctrine of Scripture, but it is not the teaching here. The passage means "once for all" in the sense of—all at once, or only once, for all time.

Just as a man might say, "I gave up my whole estate once for all to my creditors, and there was an end of the matter," so, here, our

Lord Jesus Christ is said to have offered Himself up as a sacrifice once for all—that is to say, only once, and there was an end of the whole matter. His sacrifice on behalf of His people was for all the sins before He came. Think of what they all were. Ages had succeeded ages, and among the various generations of men had been found criminals of the blackest hue, and crimes had been multiplied; but the prophet Isaiah said in vision concerning Christ, as he looked on all the multitude,

> *All we like sheep have gone astray; we have turned every one to his own way; and the LORD hath laid on him the iniquity of us all.*   *(Isa. 53:6)*

That was before He came. Reflect that there has been no second offering of Himself ever since, and never will be, but it was once, and that "once" did the deed. Let your mind ponder the nearly two thousand years that have passed since the offering. If the prophet were to stand here this day and look back through those many years, he would still say, "All we like sheep have gone astray; we have turned every one to his own way; and the LORD hath laid on him the iniquity of us all."

Oh, it is a wonderful concept! The sacrifice of the Lord Jesus was the reservoir into which all the sin of the human race ran, from this quarter, and that, and that, and that. All the sin of His people rolled in a torrent unto Him, and gathered as in a great lake. In Him was no sin, and yet the Lord made Him to be sin for us (2 Cor. 5:21).

You may have seen a deep mountain tarn that has been filled to the brim by innumerable streamlets from all the hillsides round about. From one side comes a torrent gushing down, and from another side there trickles from the moss that has overgrown the rock a little drip, drip, drip, that falls perpetually. Great and small tributaries all meet in the black tarn, which, after the rain, is full to the brim and ready to burst its banks. That lone lake portrays Christ, the meeting place of the sins of His people. It was all laid on Him, that from Him the penalty might be exacted. At His hands the price must be demanded for the ransom of all this multitude of sins.

The Blotting Out of Sin

And it is said that He did this *once for all*. I have no language with which to describe it, but when I look around me, I see the great load of sin, the huge, tremendous world of sin. No, no, it is greater than the world. Atlas might carry *that*,[1] but this is a weight in comparison with which the world is but the head of a pin. Mountains upon mountains, alps upon alps, are nothing, to the mighty mass of sin that I see before my mind's eye; and lo, it all falls upon the Well Beloved.

He stands beneath it, and bows under it, until the bloody sweat springs from every pore, and yet He does not yield to its weight in order to get away from the burden. It presses more heavily; it bows Him to the dust; it touches His very soul; it makes Him cry in anguish, "My God, my God, why hast thou forsaken me?" (Matt. 27:46); and yet, at the last, He lifts Himself up and flings it all away and cries, "It is finished" (John 19:30), and it is gone. There is not a wreck of it left; no, not an atom of it left. It is all gone at once, and once for all. He has borne the immeasurable weight and cast it off from His shoulders forever; and as it lies no more on Him, so also it lies no more on His people. Sin will never be mentioned against them anymore, forever. Oh, wondrous deed of Deity! Oh, mighty feat of love accomplished once for all! The Redeemer never offered Himself to death before. He never will do it again.

---

[1]Atlas: in Greek mythology, a Titan who, because of his part in a revolt against the gods, was condemned by Zeus to support the heavens upon his shoulders.

Look at it this way: the reason that it never will be done again is there is no need for it. All the sin that was laid upon Jesus is gone; all the sin of His people is forever discharged. He has borne it; the debt is paid. The handwriting of ordinances against us is nailed to His cross; the Accuser's charge is answered forever.

What, then, will we say of those who come forward and pretend that they perpetually present the body of Christ in the unbloody sacrifice of the mass? We say that no profane jest from the lip of Voltaire[2] ever had even the slightest degree of God-defiant blasphemy in it compared with the hideous insult of this horrible pretense. It is infernal. There can be nothing more intolerable than that notion, for our Lord Jesus Christ has offered Himself for sin once, and once for all; and he who dares to think of offering Him again, insults Him by acting as if that once were not enough. There would be no language of abhorrence too strong if the performers and attendants at the mass really knew what is implied in their professed act and deed. In the judgment of Christian charity we may earnestly pray, "Father, forgive them; for they know not what they do" (Luke 23:34).

---

[2]Voltaire: French writer, 1694–1778.

Our words fail and our ideas falter at the thought of the great Substitute, with all the sins of His people condensed into one black liquid and set before Him, for Him to drink. Can we think of Him as putting that cup to His lips, and drinking, drinking, drinking all the wrath, until He had drained the cup to the bottom and filled Himself with horror? Yet, He has finished the death-drink and turned the cup upside down, crying, "It is finished" (John 19:30). In one tremendous drink, the loving Lord has drained destruction dry for all His people, and there is no dreg nor drop left for any one of them, for now is the will of God accomplished—"by the which will we are sanctified through the offering of the body of Jesus Christ once for all" (Heb. 10:10). Glory be to God! Again, glory be to our God!

> He bore on the tree the sentence for me,
> And now both the Surety and sinner are
>   free.
> In the heavenly Lamb thrice happy I am;
> And my heart doth rejoice at the sound
>   of his name.

The Everlasting Result

At last I come to my third point: the everlasting result. There are several glorious results that have come about through God's eternal will and by Christ's effectual sacrifice.

The Expiation of Our Sin

The first everlasting result of this effectual carrying out of the will of God, is that now God regards His people's sin as expiated, and their persons as sanctified. Our sin is removed by expiation. Atonement has been offered, and its efficacy abides forever. There is no need for any other expiation. Believers repent bitterly, but this is not expiation. There is no penance to be exacted of them through putting away guilt. Their guilt is gone; their transgression is forgiven. The covenant is made with them, and it goes like this: "Their sins and iniquities will I remember no more" (Heb. 10:17). Their sins have, in fact, been ended, blotted out, and annihilated by the Redeemer's one sacrifice.

We Are Reconciled to God

Next, His people are reconciled to Him. There is no quarrel now between God and those who are in Christ Jesus. Peace is made between them. The middle wall that stood between them is taken away. Christ, by His one sacrifice, has made peace for all His people, and has effectually established a union that will never be broken.

> Lord Jesus, we believing
>   In thee have peace with God,
> Eternal life receiving,
>   The purchase of thy blood.
> Our curse and condemnation
>   Thou bearest in our stead;
> Secure is our salvation
>   In thee, our risen Head.

We Are Purified in Him

Moreover, they are not only accepted and reconciled, but they are also purified. The taint that was upon them is taken away. In God's sight they are regarded no more as unclean; they are no longer shut outside the camp. (See Numbers 5:1–4.) They may come to the throne of the heavenly grace when they desire to do so. God can have communion with them. He regards them as fit to stand in His courts and to be His servants, for they are purified, reconciled, and expiated through the one offering of Christ. Their admission into the closest intimacy with God could never be allowed if He did not regard them as purged from all uncleanness, and this has been effected not at all by themselves, but alone by the great sacrifice.

> Thy blood, not mine, O Christ,
> Thy blood so freely spilt,
> Has blanched my blackest stains,
> And purged away my guilt.
>
> Thy righteousness, O Christ,
> Alone does cover me;
> No righteousness avails
> Save that which is in thee.

Living as a Sanctified Christian

Again, what has come of this offering of Christ's body? That is the point. Let us now leave the doctrine and try to bring out the practical experience arising from it. What Christ has done in the carrying out of the great will of God has brought about salvation for all His chosen people. However, this is applied to them actually and experientially by the Holy Spirit dwelling in them, by which indwelling they know they are God's people. The Israelites were God's people, after a fashion; the Levites were especially so; and the priests were still more especially so; and these had to present perpetual sacrifices and offerings, that God might be able to look upon them as His people, for they were a sinful people.

Truly His People

You and I are not a type, but we are truly and really His people. Through Jesus Christ's offering of Himself once for all, we are really set apart to be the Lord's people, henceforth and forever. And He says of us—of as many as have believed in Jesus, and to whom the Holy Spirit has revealed His finished work—"I will be their God, and they shall be my people" (2 Cor. 6:16).

You, believers, are sanctified in this sense: you are now the ones set apart unto God, and you belong wholly to Him. Will you think that over? "I am now not my own. I do not belong now to the common order of men, as all the rest of men do. I am set apart. I am called out. I am taken aside. I am one of the Lord's own. I am His treasure and His portion. He has, through Jesus Christ's death, made me one of those of whom He says, '[They] shall dwell alone, and shall not be reckoned among the nations' (Num. 23:9)."

I want you to feel it, so that you may live under the power of that fact; I want you to feel,

"My Lord has cleansed me. My Lord has made expiation for me. My Lord has reconciled me unto God, and I am God's man, or I am God's woman. I cannot live as sinners do. I cannot be one among you. I must come out, and I must be separate (2 Cor. 6:17). I cannot find my pleasure where you find yours. I cannot find my treasure where you find yours. I am God's, and God is mine. That wondrous transaction on the cross— that wondrous unspeakable deed upon the cross—that wonderful life and death of Jesus, has made me one of God's people, set apart unto Him, and I must live as such."

Fit for His Service

When you realize that you are one of God's people, the next thing is to reflect that God, in sanctifying a people, set them apart for His service, and He made them fit for His service. You, beloved, through Christ's one great offering of His body for you, are permitted now to be a servant of God.

You know it is an awful thing for a man to try to serve God until God gives Him that right: otherwise, there is a presumption about it. Well, suppose that one of the enemies of this country, who has sought the life of our leader and has always spoken against him, were to say, "My intention is to be one of his servants; I will go into his house, and I will serve him," having all the while in his heart a rebellious, proud spirit. His service could not be tolerated; it would be sheer impudence. Even so, "Unto the wicked God saith, What hast thou to do to declare my statutes?" (Ps. 50:16).

A wicked man, pretending to serve God, does what Korah, Dathan, and Abiram tried to do when they rebelled against Moses (see Numbers 16): he will try to offer incense, yet he is not purified and not called to the work, and he has no fitness for it. But now, beloved, you who are in Christ are called to be His servant. You have permission and leave to serve Him. It ought to be your great joy to be an accepted servant of the living God. If you are only the Lord's chimney sweep, you have a greater privilege than if you were an emperor on earth.

If the highest thing you ever will be allowed to do, should be to untie the laces of your Master's shoe, or to wash His servants' feet—if the master is Christ, then you are favored above the mightiest of the mighty. Men of renown may envy you; their Order of the Garter[3] is nothing compared with the high

---

[3]Order of the Garter: the highest English Order of Chivalry, and one of the most important of all such Orders throughout the world.

dignity of being a servant of King Jesus. Look upon this as being the result of Christ's death upon the cross, that a poor, sinful creature like you, who was once a slave of the Devil, is now allowed to be the servant of God. On the cross my Master bought for us a sanctification that has made us the Lord's people, and has enabled us to engage in His service. Do we not rejoice in this?

Acceptable in His Sight

Next to that we have this privilege, that what we do can now be accepted. Because Jesus Christ, by the offering of His body once, has perfected the Father's will and has sanctified us, what we do is now acceptable to God. Previously, we might have done whatever we wanted to, but God would not have accepted it from a sinner's hands—from the hands of one who was out of Christ. Now He accepts anything from us.

You dropped a penny into the offering: it was all that you could give, and the Lord accepted it. It dropped into His hand. You offered a little prayer in the middle of business this afternoon because you heard an ill word spoken, and your God accepted that prayer. You went down the street and spoke to a poor sick person: you did not say much, but you said all you could, and the great God accepted it.

Acceptance by the Beloved, not only for our persons, but also for our prayers and our work, is one of the sweetest things I know. We are accepted. That is the joy of it. Through that one great, bloody sacrifice, once for all offered, God's people are forever accepted, and what His people do for Him is accepted, too. And now we are privileged to the highest degree, being sanctified—that is to say, made into God's people, God's servants, and God's accepted servants. Every privilege that we could have had if we had never sinned, is now ours, and we are in Him as His children. We have more than would have come to us by the covenant of works; and if we will but know it, and live up to it, even the very privilege of suffering and the privilege of being tried, the privilege of being in need, should be looked upon as a great gift.

An angel spirit, seated high alone there, meditating and adoring, might say to himself, "I have served God: these swift wings have borne me through the heavens on His errands, but I have never suffered for Him. I have never been despised for Him. Drunkards have never called me evil names. I have never been misrepresented as God's servant. After all, though I have served Him, it has been one perpetual joy. He has set a hedge about me and all that I have (Job 1:10)."

If an angel could envy anybody, I think he would envy the martyr who had the privilege of burning to death for Christ. Or, he would envy Job, who, when stripped of everything and covered with sores, could sit on a dunghill and still honor his God. Such men as these achieved a service unique within itself, which has sparkling diamonds of the finest clarity and luster glittering about it—the kind that cannot be found in a ministry without suffering, complete as it may be. You are favored sons of Adam, you who have become sons of God. You are favored beyond cherubim and seraphim in accomplishing a service for the manifestation of the riches of the grace of God, which unfallen spirits never could accomplish. Rejoice and be exceedingly glad that this one offering has put you there!

Eternally Secure

And now you are eternally secure. No sin can ever be laid at your door, for it is all put away; and sin being removed, every other evil has lost its fang and sting. Now you are eternally beloved, for you are one with Him who can never be other than dear to the heart of Jehovah. That union never can be broken, for nothing can separate us from the love of God (Rom. 8:38–39); and therefore, your security can never be imperiled.

You are now in some measure glorified, for "the spirit of glory and of God resteth upon you" (1 Pet. 4:14), and "our conversation is in heaven; from whence also we look for the Saviour, the Lord Jesus Christ" (Phil. 3:20), who "hath [already] raised us up together, and made us sit together in heavenly places" (Eph. 2:6). Heaven is already ours in promise, in price, and in principle, and the preparation for it has also begun.

> All that remains for me
> Is but to love and sing,
> And wait until the angels come
> To bear me to their King.

In such a spirit would I always live.

Brother or sister, are you discouraged at this time? Do you have a great trouble upon you? Are you alone in the world? Do others misjudge you, or does the sword of scandal pierce your very soul? Do fierce coals of juniper (see Psalm 120:4) await those vicious tongues that wrong you? Do you feel "bowed down to the dust" (Ps. 44:25)? Yet, what position are you in to be despairing? Child of God, and heir of all things, "why art thou cast down" (Ps. 42:5)? Joint heir with Christ, why do you abase yourself? Why do you lie among the pots (see Psalm 68:13) when you already have angels' wings upon you?

Get up! Your heritage is not here among the dragons and the owls. (See Job 30:29.) Up! You are one of God's eagles, born for brighter light than earth could bear—light that would blind the bleary-eyed sons of men if they were once to get a veiled glimpse of it. You, a twice-born man, one of the imperial family, one who will sit upon a throne with Christ as surely as Christ sits there (see Revelation 3:21), what position are you in, that you are moaning and groaning?

Wipe your eyes and smooth your brow, and in the strength of the Eternal, go to your life battle. It will not be long. The trumpet of victory almost sounds in your ears. Will you now retreat? No, for you can win the day. "Trust in the LORD, and do good; so shalt thou dwell in the land, and verily thou shalt be fed" (Ps. 37:3), until He comes to catch you away. There you will see what Jesus did for you when He made His body once for all a sacrifice, that He might fulfill the will of the eternal Father, and sanctify you and all His people unto God forever and ever.

May the best of blessings rest upon all who are in Christ Jesus. Amen.

Appendix A

Antiochus Epiphanes, ruler of Syria and the Seleucid Dynasty from 175 to 164 B.C., intervened rather brutally in the fighting that had been troubling Jerusalem during that time. He made a great attempt to hellenize the Jews, or to assimilate the Jews into Greek culture and views, by, among other things, destroying all the Old Testament books he could find.

According to *Great Themes of the Book, Part 3,* of the *Living by the Book* series, Antiochus became virtually the Antichrist to the writer of the book of Daniel. He

> sacked Jerusalem; stripped the temple of its gold, implements, and secret treasures; and took ten thousand people into captivity as slaves. He compelled the Jews to cease worshipping God, placed idols on the altar, and sacrificed swine (an unclean animal according to Jewish dietary law) to them. He erected similar shrines in every Jewish city and village and forbade the practice of circumcision. Mothers who disobeyed were tied to crosses, strangled, and had their sons hung about their necks.

Because offering a sow on the altar was the sacrificing of an unclean animal for a sin offering, Antiochus desecrated the purity of the temple with his sacrifice. His action is considered by many to be the initial historical fulfillment of the first prophecies regarding the abomination of desolation. (See Daniel 11:31.) The "awful death" of Antiochus, of which Spurgeon writes, was due to an illness in the year 164 B.C.

Appendix B

Chapter 13 of the Baptist Confession of Faith, entitled, "Of Sanctification," concerns the work of the Holy Spirit in sanctification. The following are the three points from that chapter.

A. They who are united to Christ, effectually called, and regenerated, having a new heart and a new spirit created in them through the virtue of Christ's death and resurrection, are also further sanctified, really and personally, through the same virtue, by His Word and Spirit dwelling in them; the dominion of the whole body of sin is destroyed, and the several lusts thereof are more and more weakened and mortified, and they [are] more and more quickened and strengthened in all saving graces, to the practice of all true holiness, without which no man shall see the Lord. (See Acts 20:32; Romans 6:5–6; John 17:17; Ephesians 3:16–19; 1 Thessalonians 5:21–23; Romans 6:14; Galatians 5:24; Colossians 1:11; 2 Corinthians 7:1; Hebrews 12:14.)

B. This sanctification is throughout the whole man, yet imperfect in this life; there abideth still some remnants of corruption in every part, whence ariseth a continual and irreconcilable war; the flesh lusting against the Spirit, and the Spirit against the flesh. (See 1 Thessalonians 5:23; Romans 7:18, 23; Galatians 5:17; 1 Peter 2:11.)

C. In which war, although the remaining corruption for a time may much prevail, yet through the continual supply of strength from the sanctifying Spirit of Christ, the regenerate part doth overcome; and so the saints grow in grace, perfecting holiness in the fear of God, pressing after an heavenly life, in evangelical obedience to all the commands which Christ, as Head and King, in His Word, hath prescribed them. (See Romans 7:23; 6:14; Ephesians 4:15–16; 2 Corinthians 3:18; 7:1.)